IMAGES
of America

ZION NATIONAL PARK

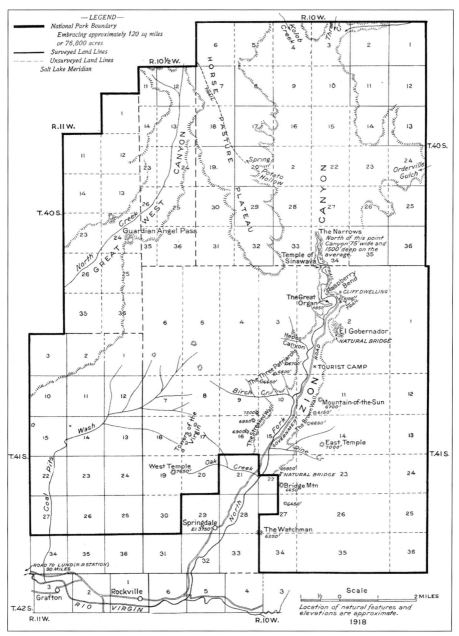

On March 18, 1918, Pres. Woodrow Wilson signed a proclamation changing the previously named Mukuntuweap National Monument in southern Utah to Zion National Park and enlarging its area to 120 square miles. On November 20, 1919, a bill officially establishing "Zion Park in the State of Utah" was signed by President Wilson. This 1918 National Park Service map shows the prospective park boundaries. (Author's collection.)

ON THE COVER: A tradition during the early years of the Utah Parks Company's operations at Zion National Park was the "sing-a-way" presented to departing tour buses by waitresses at the Zion Lodge. (Photograph from the Utah Parks Company Collection, Southern Utah University, Cedar City, Utah.)

IMAGES
of America

ZION NATIONAL
PARK

Tiffany Taylor

ARCADIA
PUBLISHING

Published by Arcadia Publishing
Charleston SC, Chicago IL, Portsmouth NH, San Francisco CA

Printed in the United States of America

Library of Congress Catalog Card Number: 2008928360

For all general information contact Arcadia Publishing at:
Telephone 843-853-2070
Fax 843-853-0044
E-mail sales@arcadiapublishing.com
For customer service and orders:
Toll-Free 1-888-313-2665

Visit us on the Internet at www.arcadiapublishing.com

To my grandfather, Hal L. Taylor,
a former seasonal park ranger at Zion National Park
who inspired me to follow in his footsteps;
and to my great-aunt, Elsa F. Ruesch,
formerly a secretary to the superintendent of the park,
whose door was always open to my family
and me during our many trips to Zion.

CONTENTS

ACKNOWLEDGMENTS

First and foremost, I would like to thank my parents, Steven and Diane Taylor, for their encouragement and support throughout my life and for their help with this project. It was quite a challenge to complete this book while attending graduate school, and I could not have done it without their willingness to help gather information and proofread my work. Thank you, Mom and Dad! I also want to thank Dr. Susan Sessions Rugh, professor of history and associate dean for the College of Family, Home, and Social Sciences at Brigham Young University, who gave me the idea for the subject matter of this book and encouraged me throughout the process of compiling photographs and information. I am grateful to my editors, Hannah Carney and Jared Jackson with Arcadia Publishing, for their patience and assistance. Thanks to Stephen C. Bern of LaVerkin, Utah, for the hours he spent scanning, digitizing, and skillfully restoring photographs from the J. L. Crawford Collection. I would like to thank author and historian J. L. Crawford for his permission to use his father's photographs in this book. I am grateful to Sylvia Frye, museum specialist at the National Park Service Harpers Ferry Center, for her timely assistance in scanning photographs from the NPS Historic Photograph Collection. My appreciation goes out to Janet Seegmiller at Southern Utah University's Gerald R. Sherratt Library for helping me acquire photographs from the Utah Parks Collection and to Fay Cope and Kristine Young for their support and helpful suggestions. I would also like to thank Denise Halverson Williams and her husband, David Williams, for generously allowing me to use photographs, documents, and histories from the late Alta Jolley Halverson's collection. I appreciate the added assistance of Della Crawford Higley, Nellie Hardy Ballard, and Flora Anderson Ruesch, who spent time sharing with me their memories of life in Springdale and Zion Canyon and allowed me to scan photographs from their collections. Their stories are the stories of Zion National Park, and I hope to do them justice in the pages that follow.

INTRODUCTION

Zion National Park's natural and cultural history is preserved in its rocks. Layers of sedimentary rock reveal millions of years of geological change. The canyon, once covered by an ocean, has since been shaped by volcanic eruptions and earthquakes and continues to be carved by the flowing waters of the Virgin River. Dinosaur tracks are imprinted in riverbed shale, and pictorial records of Native American inhabitants are etched into the canyon walls. Surviving sandstone buildings help chart the evolution of the area from a secluded canyon to a national park and tourist destination.

After it was settled by Mormon pioneers in the early 1860s, the scenic wonders of the region were officially recognized by Pres. William Howard Taft with the creation of Mukuntuweap National Monument in 1909. Due to the poor condition of roads in the area, however, access to the national monument by the general public was limited. By 1917, a passable road to Zion Canyon was completed, and that same year, William Wylie established the area's first tourist accommodations, known as the Wylie Way Camp. In 1918, the area under government jurisdiction was expanded to 120 square miles, and in 1919, Mukuntuweap National Monument officially became known as Zion National Park with the passing of Senate Bill 8282. The park was dedicated on September 15, 1920, becoming Utah's first national park. Approximately 3,692 visitors came to the newly created national park that year, and by 1930, the number of visitors had increased to more than 55,000.

By 1922, the Union Pacific Railroad had established a railhead in Cedar City, Utah, just over 50 miles from the entrance to Zion. Union Pacific then organized a subsidiary company, the Utah Parks Company, to develop tourist access to and accommodations in the national park. The Utah Parks Company purchased the Wylie Camp, and by 1925, architect Gilbert Stanley Underwood had completed the Zion Lodge. From 1927 to 1930, the Zion–Mount Caramel Highway and Tunnel projects were undertaken. As the park became increasingly accessible and the scenic wonders of southern Utah were voiced abroad, the number of tourists steadily increased. Annual park visitation numbers broke the one million mark in 1975, the two million mark in 1990, and Zion National Park now sees annual visitation numbers regularly surpassing 2.5 million.

Some of my earliest and fondest childhood memories include family road trips to Zion National Park. My dad would tell us stories about driving tour buses through the narrow Zion Tunnel when he was employed by the Utah Parks Company as a young man. He would tell us about the sandstone house near the east entrance to the park where he and his family lived while Grandpa Taylor was a seasonal park ranger at Zion. When we drove into Springdale, the town located at the mouth of Zion Canyon, we would stop to visit my dad's aunt, Elsa Ruesch, a longtime Springdale resident and former park employee. We would then go down Aunt Elsa's driveway to a rustic cabin—the lone remnant of an old motel—where we would stay for a few days. My family and I have always enjoyed hiking at Zion, biking at Zion, and driving through the tunnel with the car windows rolled down. A rite of passage for my siblings and me took place when, as teenagers, we were deemed ready to hike to the top of Angels Landing. In the evenings, we would walk from the cabin to downtown Springdale to buy ice cream at the market. The landscape of Springdale and Zion National Park has changed somewhat since my family first started taking frequent trips there, but I realize that even the Zion of my childhood was much changed from the early days of exploration, settlement, and tourist development in the area. A number of tokens of Zion's past remain—the deteriorating wooden frame of the old cable works atop Cable Mountain, petroglyphs carved into the rocks, and several original Park Service buildings—but much of the history of Zion National Park is preserved only through the stories and pictures of the people who saw, with their own eyes (or through their own camera lens), the history of the park unfold.

Many of the photographs in this book come from the personal collections of those who were born and raised in or near Zion National Park. J. L. Crawford was born on his parents' homestead in Zion Canyon and spent his childhood on the family farm. His father, William Louis Crawford, was a pioneer photographer in the area and captured many of the stunning images that follow. Della Crawford Higley is the niece of the first acting park superintendent, Walter Ruesch. Flora Anderson Ruesch, widow of Rupert Ruesch, is Walter Ruesch's daughter-in-law. Nellie Hardy Ballard's father, Alvin C. Hardy, first came to Springdale in 1927 and thereafter ran a market and post office in town. Nellie remembers growing up with Zion National Park as her playground. Denise Halverson Williams's mother, Alta Jolley Halverson, was the daughter of Donal Jolley, the first official chief ranger at Zion National Park. The Jolley family resided at Zion until 1943, when their father was transferred to Lake Mead National Recreation Area. Through the pictures and stories of these generous people, the history of Zion National Park becomes more than a list of names and dates—it becomes a saga of discovery, perseverance, and growth.

One

TREASURE OF THE GODS

Long before human intervention began to shape the landscape of Zion Canyon, natural forces were at work. Layers of sedimentary rock containing sandstone, shale, petrified wood, volcanic ash, fossilized bone, siltstone, and limestone reveal immense geographical, biological, and climatic changes over time.

It is assumed that the earliest inhabitants of the region were small groups of hunter-gatherers whose archaeological evidence dates back to 6,000 BC. By 3,000 BC, evidence suggests that groups of Native Americans known as Basketmakers began to cultivate corn and squash along rivers and streams. Later, from AD 500 to AD 1300, two horticultural groups, the Virgin Anasazi and the Parowan Fremont, appear. Around AD 1300, both groups disappear from the archaeological record of Zion quite suddenly. Possible causes of their disappearance include devastating droughts and floods that would have made farming very difficult. The next group to appear in the region was the Southern Paiute. It was the Paiute Indians who were encountered by early explorers in the region, such as Franciscan missionaries Silvestre Vélez de Escalante and Francisco Atanasio Domínguez, who passed through the area in 1776; trapper Jedediah Strong Smith, who followed the Domínguez-Escalante route in 1826; explorer John Charles Frémont, who crossed the Virgin River in 1844; and John Wesley Powell, a soldier, geologist, and explorer who surveyed Zion Canyon in 1872. Mormon pioneers who explored the area in the late 1850s also noted the presence of the Paiute Indians.

It is from the early Native American inhabitants of Zion Canyon that many of the place names were drawn. John Wesley Powell recorded, "The Indians call the canyon through which the river runs, Mu-koon-tu-weap, or Straight Canyon." Early settlers in the area interpreted the word *Mukuntuweap* to mean "the place of the gods." Though interpretations of the word varied, Native Americans, explorers, and settlers recognized the sanctity of the canyon's scenery. It truly appeared to be a hidden treasure of the gods.

In 1882, surveyor Clarence Dutton traveled to southern Utah and recorded, "In an instant, there flashed before us a scene never to be forgotten." He noted two distinct "temples" of stone on either side of the canyon. Shown here is the stone peak known as Steamboat Mountain to early settlers but which, after Dutton's description, adopted the name West Temple. (Photograph by William L. Crawford; courtesy of J. L. Crawford.)

Across the Virgin River from West Temple stands the Watchman—an imposing 6,555-foot peak standing watch over Springdale and the entrance to Zion National Park. (Photograph by William L. Crawford; courtesy of J. L. Crawford.)

Though Zion National Park is located in a desert climate, winters still typically bring snow to the mountain peaks. This winter scene features the Watchman, originally called Flanigan Peak by Springdale residents in recognition of the Flanigan family, whose farm was located at the base of the mountain. While the origin of the name "Watchman" is not certain, the title may have been given to the mountain by Frederick Vining Fisher, a Methodist minister from Ogden, Utah, who was accompanied by two young men from the town of Rockville, Utah, when he visited the park in September 1916. The party reportedly decided to assign names—which soon caught on with the general public—to various mountains as they traveled through the canyon. (Photograph by William L. Crawford; courtesy of J. L. Crawford.)

Seen here looking south (left) and north (below) is the Virgin River, a 200-mile tributary of the Colorado River, which has, for centuries, carved and shaped Zion Canyon. In 1776, the Domínguez-Escalante party crossed the river and called it Rio Sulfurio—the sulphur river. It may have been named Rio Virgin by Spanish or Mexican traders traveling along the Old Spanish Trail. Another theory claims the river was named after Thomas Virgin, a member of Jedediah Smith's 1827 team of explorers, although Smith himself called it the Adams River in honor of Pres. John Quincy Adams. In 1844, Capt. John C. Frémont described the Virgin as "the most dreary river" he had ever seen. (Left, photograph from the Alta J. Halverson collection, courtesy of Denise H. Williams; below, photograph by William L. Crawford, courtesy of J. L. Crawford.)

This view of Zion Canyon clearly shows the winding path of the Virgin River. The Domínguez-Escalante party noted irrigation ditches and fields of corn along the river—presumably planted by the Paiute Indians. Escalante wrote in October 1776, "From here down the stream and on the mesa and on both sides for a long distance, according to what we learned, these Indians apply themselves to the cultivation of maize and calabashes." Native Americans called the river Pa'rus, or Pahroos, appropriately meaning rushing water or a dirty, turbulent stream. Meteorologist and historian J. Cecil Alter, who composed a number of travelogues in the first half of the 20th century, wrote, "The River was never a virgin at any known age, for each springtime when the gallant Kolob is doffing its cap of snow to the returning sun, the jealous Virgin becomes a dirty, carousing she-devil for sure. Moreover, the fickle lady is prone to go on a little spree after every summer thundershower of importance on the plateau." (Photograph from the Alta J. Halverson collection; courtesy of Denise H. Williams.)

Sixteen-year-old Claud Hirschi and his friend by the name of Bingham, both from Rockville, are credited with naming the Great Organ, a distinctive peak jutting out of the Big Bend of the Virgin River. Hirschi and Bingham were Frederick Vining Fisher's guides when Fisher toured Zion in 1916. Naturalist and historian Angus M. Woodbury wrote that at one point Hirschi and Bingham paused in front of a particular mountain. When Fisher asked why the boys had stopped, they said that they were "waiting for the organist to come and play The Great Organ." (Photograph by William L. Crawford; courtesy of J. L. Crawford.)

Hidden Canyon features sandstone ravines, steep canyon walls, and sheer cliffs. It was in canyons like this that Wai-no-pits, an evil supernatural entity in Paiute tradition, was believed to dwell. Early settlers noted that the resident Native Americans always seemed to avoid the canyon after nightfall. This was because the Paiutes believed that Wai-no-pits lurked in darkness and shadows. In the supernatural hierarchy of the Paiutes, the Wolf God, or Sin-na'wava, was the main spirit, and a spirit known as Kai-ne-sava was a mysterious entity of changeable moods. According to Paiute belief, it was Kai-ne-sava who was responsible for pushing large boulders down the canyon or building fires on mountain peaks. John Wesley Powell once remarked, "When a raven perches on a rock near by and wistfully searches with his eye for a stray morsel of food, the Indian says the Kai-ni-suv has come, and the children are forbidden to drive it away." (National Park Service photograph; courtesy of Della C. Higley.)

In a description of Zion, J. Cecil Alter wrote, "The canyon is formed by a magnificent palisade of sandstone pillars and front walls a half mile high, of rare beauty of form and great richness of color. The flat tops of the perpendicular pillars are largely capped with unique woodlands in cloudland, like inaccessible Babylonian gardens in midair." (Photograph from the Alta J. Halverson collection; courtesy of Denise H. Williams.)

Alter described West Temple as being "the most conspicuous figure in the park." Of the mountain, he wrote, "Its elliptical shape, bulging sides and turreted top give it some of the lines of an immense ship, riding high." The turreted top of West Temple is visible at the left side of this photograph. (Photograph from the Alta J. Halverson collection; courtesy of Denise H. Williams.)

This photograph, taken atop Observation Point in 1929 by George A. Grant, shows horse wrangler Walter Beatty with a park visitor. Towering over the peak known as Angels Landing, the overlook on the East Rim of the canyon offers a stunning view across to the Great White Throne (shown on the left side of the picture). (Courtesy of the National Park Service History Collection, Harpers Ferry Center.)

The Great White Throne (here in 1959) was named by Frederick Vining Fisher, who wrote, "I have looked for this mountain all my life but never expected to find it in this world. This is The Great White Throne." Perhaps the most iconic of Zion's peaks, the 2,000-foot-tall sandstone mountain was featured on a 1934 postage stamp. (Author's collection.)

The name of Angels Landing, a distinctive mountain peak across the Virgin River from the Great White Throne, is also attributed to Frederick Fisher, who remarked that "the Angels would never land on the Throne, but would reverently pause at the foot." J. Cecil Alter likewise observed, "At Big Bend, alias Raspberry Bend, six miles from the canyon entrance, the river flows around the Angel's Landing promontory on the west, washing the feet of Observation Point, Cable Mountain, the Great White Throne, Mount Majestic, the President, and other celebrated skyscrapers which serrate the puckered skyline." Angels Landing rises 1,500 feet above the canyon floor, and the hike to its crest is one of the most popular at Zion. Hikers follow an exhilarating trail along the spine of the mountain, with deep chasms and sheer cliffs lining their path. The final stretch of the trail to the top ascends nearly 500 feet in just one-and-a-half miles. (Photograph by the author.)

Former National Park Service naturalist Allen Hagood observed that "Zion's foundation stones are conspicuously tabular, and the rock stands out in flat-lying layers" etched by gravity and running water. The distinctive rock formations created by this natural process of erosion are exemplified by the picture below, which features the Sentinel peak, the Beehives, and the Streaked Wall. More than 3,500 years ago, a massive landslide from this mountain blocked the Virgin River, but the river found its way around the slide, leaving behind the Sand Bench. (Photographs from the Alta J. Halverson collection; courtesy of Denise H. Williams.)

This photograph, taken from Blacks Canyon, features Bridge Mountain, named for the natural arch or "flying buttress" on its face. The mountain was originally named Crawford Peak because it is located directly east of the original Crawford homestead and the Crawford farm encompassed its lower slopes. (Photograph by William L. Crawford; courtesy of J. L. Crawford.)

Shown here is Oliver D. Gifford's home, which once sat in the Virgin River floodplain within view of Zion's towering peaks. In contrast to the stone spires, horizontal layers of eroded sedimentary rock line the lowlands of Zion Canyon. (Photograph by William L. Crawford; courtesy of J. L. Crawford.)

Checkerboard Mesa, at the east entrance to the park, is appropriately named with its vertical weather cracks and lines of horizontal bedding planes. Zion National Park has many unique natural features, and it is no wonder that the canyon's first inhabitants, the Native Americans, deferred to the supernatural in an attempt to explain its creation. (Photograph from the Alta J. Halverson collection; courtesy of Denise H. Williams.)

Pictured here are, from left to right, D. Kelley, J. Edgemond, and D. Chick reconstructing the remains of a Native American granary as part of an Eagle Scout project in 1929. While the physical remnants of Zion's early inhabitants are few, ancient stories and traditions are preserved in the canyon's rocks along with the natural history of the park. (Courtesy of the National Park Service History Collection, Harpers Ferry Center.)

Two

THE PIONEERING SPIRIT

Mormon pioneers first arrived in the Great Basin region of the western United States in 1847. As these settlers sought to establish communities supported by self-sufficiency, it is not surprising that Brigham Young wanted to utilize the mineral-rich regions in the southern tier of what would, in 1896, become the state of Utah. The climate in Utah's "Dixie" was conducive to growing cotton, and it was hoped that enough cotton could be harvested to supply the needs of church members throughout the region. Facing a scarcity of water, families sent to settle the area and establish the "Cotton Mission" in 1857 were drawn to the banks of the Virgin River, a tributary of the Colorado River. Here they faced a conundrum—the river made farming possible through irrigation, but at the same time, its violent and unpredictable floods posed a constant threat to their crops. Life was hard for these early settlers, and they found it was a challenge to sustain themselves and their families.

In 1861, another group of settlers was sent to assist those already living in southern Utah. Towns such as Springdale, Rockville, Grafton, and Virgin City were soon established, as families found ways to subsist despite the harsh environment. Ursula C. Gifford raised silkworms in Springdale. Cornelia Crawford grew peas and sold them for seed. Large orchards were planted, and some cotton was grown. One of the resources the settlers wanted to utilize was the timber found in the mountains. Their ingenuity was shown in the construction of a cable works to transport lumber from high elevations down to the river valley. Though the Cotton Mission never proved to be a great economic success, it did set in motion the settlement of southern Utah as the determined pioneers established and maintained a presence in the desert region.

Early settlers in the towns of Springdale, Rockville, Oak Creek, Duncan's Retreat, Northrop, Shunesburg, and Grafton formed close bonds as they worked together to survive harsh conditions. Pictured above in 1904 is a group of Springdale residents on an excursion up the canyon to Weeping Rock. (Photograph by William L. Crawford; courtesy of J. L. Crawford.)

First settled by Mormon pioneers in 1862, the town of Springdale had grown noticeably by 1915. It featured a number of frame homes and wooden barns, and its location at the mouth of Zion Canyon offered residents and visitors a stunning panoramic view of the surrounding mountains. (Photograph by William L. Crawford; courtesy of J. L. Crawford.)

The town of Springdale had been surveyed in 1863, and a post office was established in 1897. The first store was set up by Johann J. Ruesch in 1908. Pictured here in 1935, Springdale experienced significant growth in a relatively short amount of time. (Photograph by William L. Crawford; courtesy of J. L. Crawford.)

The area where the entrance to Zion National Park is now located was once known as Oak Creek Village. It was in Oak Creek that several pioneer families settled. One of these settlers was William R. Crawford, whose property extended to the base of what locals called Crawford Peak. (Courtesy of Nellie H. Ballard.)

In 1851, Carnelia Gifford was born in Manti, Utah, to Samuel Kendall Gifford and Lora Ann DeMille. She married William Robinson Crawford on November 1, 1868, in Shunesburg. William was born in Illinois in 1842, the son of John Crawford and Marilla Terry. William and Carnelia Crawford were two of the earliest settlers in Utah's Dixie after they answered Brigham Young's call to colonize the area. (Courtesy of Denise H. Williams.)

In 1879, William Robinson Crawford moved his family from Rockville to Oak Creek. He and Carnelia raised 11 children to adulthood at their homestead, pictured here in 1920. This land was later purchased by the federal government and became part of Zion National Park. (Photograph by William L. Crawford; courtesy of J. L. Crawford.)

Pictured here is the Crawford family. The individual photographs include parents William and Carnelia (in the center at the top of the page), and following in a counterclockwise direction are sons John, Louis, Samuel, James, Daniel, Jake, and Joseph, and daughters Emma, Marilla, Mary, Fanny, and Annie. Another daughter, Lora Ann, who died when she was only 16 months old, is not pictured. The Crawfords were known as a hardworking family, and Carnelia once described them as "the happiest family in the whole valley." When the Crawfords had first moved to southern Utah, the extent of their possessions included one plate, knife, fork, spoon, cup, and a Dutch oven. Through their thriftiness and hard work, however, William and Carnelia established a comfortable home for their family. (Photograph from the William L. Crawford collection; courtesy of J. L. Crawford.)

With the majestic canyon as their backdrop, Carnelia Gifford Crawford and her daughters pose in front of Walter Ruesch's 1926 Chevrolet. The daughters are, from left to right, Annie, Mary, Marilla, Fanny, and Emma. Annie married George Isom and had 11 children; Mary married Marion Fisk Stout and had 15 children; Marilla married Walter Ruesch and had seven children; Fanny married John Jones Gifford and had 13 children, and Emma married Samuel Bell in her later years and had no children. (Photograph by William L. Crawford; courtesy of J. L. Crawford.)

Crawford Homestead Springdale, Utah looking South.

William R. Crawford purchased his Oak Creek homestead from Joseph Millett. After living on the property for 10 years, William tore down the original two-room house and built a four-room, two-story home for his family using lumber that he transported 110 miles from Mount Trumbull, Arizona. He was a skilled workman and ran a successful farm. A smokehouse was built on the property, alfalfa was grown in the fields, and an extensive fruit orchard was planted. During the winter, apples and vegetables were stored in pits outside of the Crawford home, and watermelons and squash were stored under the house. William and Carnelia's daughter Annie C. Isom remembered her father "making our brooms, tubs, furniture, molasses barrels, and several gadgets for our kitchen." As his 11 surviving children grew to adulthood, William Crawford divided his Oak Creek homestead, pictured here, among them. (Photograph by William L. Crawford; courtesy of J. L. Crawford.)

Pictured here are two of William and Carnelia's sons. William Louis (left), who went by the name Louis, married Mary Jane Bean and had seven children. James (right) married Paulina Ruesch and had eight children. (Photograph from the William L. Crawford collection; courtesy of J. L. Crawford.)

Louis Crawford was born to Carnelia Gifford and William Robinson Crawford on July 15, 1873, in Rockville, Utah. He was married at age 36 after serving a mission to Oklahoma for the Church of Jesus Christ of Latter-day Saints. (Photograph from the William L. Crawford collection; courtesy of J. L. Crawford.)

Louis became fond of photography and took his camera equipment with him wherever he went. This photograph shows him with his trusted sheepdog and rifle on one of his many sheepherding expeditions. The lines penned below the photograph begin with the words, "Oh solitudes." (Photograph from the William L. Crawford collection; courtesy of J. L. Crawford.)

Louis was able to take photographs of himself by using a spool of thread to trip the shutter on his camera. This self-portrait shows his "sheep camp"—the name he gave to the campsites he set up while out herding sheep and goats. (Photograph from the William L. Crawford collection; courtesy of J. L. Crawford.)

Louis Crawford became one of the earliest photographers of the Zion landscape. After marrying and having children, he kept a darkroom in his family's home where he produced hundreds of stunning black-and-white photographs of the canyon, its residents, and its visitors. (Photograph from the William L. Crawford collection; courtesy of J. L. Crawford.)

A popular photographic form during the late 19th and early 20th centuries was the stereograph (below). These double images were captured using a twin-lens camera and were then mounted on cards designed for use with a stereographic viewer to offer a three-dimensional view of the scene depicted in the photograph. Stereographs of Zion, like the one pictured here, became popular tokens for tourists. (Author's collection.)

This self-portrait was taken by Louis Crawford when he and Mary Jane Bean were on their honeymoon in Zion Canyon. The photographic equipment of Louis Crawford's time had been improved since the early days of photography, but taking pictures still required a great deal of skill and was a time-consuming process. The process of taking a picture included careful placement of the camera and then the insertion into a holder of a glass plate coated with a light-sensitive solution that had been mixed in a darkroom. The holder was then placed in the camera, and an exposure was made. The plate was developed in a portable darkroom—usually a light-proof tent. Exposure time was usually between five seconds and three minutes. After photographs were taken in the field, the photographer would typically return to a permanent darkroom and prepare prints from the glass-plate negatives. (Photograph from the William L. Crawford collection; courtesy of J. L. Crawford.)

Pictured above is a view of the barnyard on the Crawford homestead. Louis and Mary Crawford raised their family on 360 acres of the original homestead. Their children were Elva, Lloyd, J. L., Ladessa, Bulah, Beth, and Lilly. Pictured below is the Louis Crawford family out for a picnic in the canyon. Louis and Mary were both hard workers. Mary supervised the family garden and the raising of chickens, while Louis worked in the family orchards. William Louis Crawford died in 1935 at the age of 62. His photographs provide a lasting record of his family and the landscape of Zion National Park. (Photographs by William L. Crawford; courtesy of J. L. Crawford.)

Louis Crawford's brother James was born on January 10, 1877, in Rockville, Utah. On March 15, 1898, he married Paulina Ruesch in St. George, Utah. Pictured here with their oldest son, John (whom the family called "Jay"), the couple settled in Oak Creek Village, where James built a three-room home. (Photograph from the Alta J. Halverson collection; courtesy of Denise H. Williams.)

Paulina Ruesch was born to Elisa Spiess and Johann Jakob Ruesch on January 20, 1880, in Toquerville, Utah. James Crawford never paid much attention to young Paulina until he was captivated by her singing voice one Sunday at church. Her daughter Della C. Higley remembered that Paulina had "a beautiful voice and a sunny disposition." (Photograph from the Alta J. Halverson collection; courtesy of Denise Halverson Williams.)

Paulina Ruesch Crawford's parents, Johann Jakob Ruesch and Elisa Spiess, were both born in Switzerland. Johann was born on January 24, 1845, to Johannes Ruesch and Anna Barbara Banziger. Elisa Spiess was born on September 29, 1845, to Johannes Spiess and Annetta Kunzle. The couple was married and had three boys before they joined the Church of Jesus Christ of Latter-day Saints and decided to move to America. They settled in St. George, Utah, and Johann assisted in the construction of the St. George LDS Temple. The family then moved to Toquerville and later to Springdale. (Both, courtesy of Flora A. Ruesch.)

After Johann Ruesch and his family settled in Springdale, he was asked by John Beatty of Toquerville if he would sell goods for him in Springdale. Johann accepted and in 1908 built a store along the main road through town. The store was later owned and operated by John A. Allred. In addition to building the store, Johann Ruesch, a skilled craftsman, built a home for his family next to the store. The Ruesch home, pictured here, still stands along Zion Boulevard in Springdale. Johann and Elisa had seven children: William, Gottlieb, Henrich, Gottfried, John, Paulina, and Walter. Paulina's daughter Della Crawford Higley remembered that her grandparents "had beautiful voices," and her grandma "did much yodeling." Della's brother Reuben remembered that his grandmother Elisa could start to knit a pair of socks when she left to get the mail and have them finished by the time she returned. (Courtesy of Flora A. Ruesch.)

Gottfried Ruesch was the fourth child of Johann Jakob and Elisa Spiess Ruesch and the first born in the United States. He was born in St. George, Utah, on November 16, 1874. He married Clara Elizabeth Hepworth on April 25, 1894. Clara was born on May 14, 1876, in Oxford, Idaho, to Emily Dyson and Squire Hepworth. Gottfried and Clara had 12 children. Clara died on October 28, 1925, and Gottfried on March 2, 1929. Both are buried in the Springdale Cemetery. (Both courtesy of Flora A. Ruesch.)

This Springdale house is thought to have belonged to Gottfried and Clara Ruesch. Clara's parents, Squire Hepworth and Emily Dyson, had traveled to Springdale with the second wave of settlers called by Brigham Young to southern Utah. Those chosen to inhabit the beautiful but arid land were skilled at various trades, thus making subsistence in the desert possible. Squire Hepworth was a shoemaker and made shoes for the entire community. He tanned available leather by hand and then fastened the sole to the upper part of the shoe using wooden pegs. He then sewed the leather together with Irish flax thread. Other area residents also possessed specialized skills. William R. Crawford was a noted wagon maker; John J. Allred was a doctor; Albert Petty and his sons were millers; Samuel K. and Alpheus Gifford were chair makers; Joseph Millet made sturdy baskets; and Johann Ruesch made caskets. (Courtesy of Flora A. Ruesch.)

Hyrum Ruesch, seen here in both photographs, was born to Gottfried and Clara Ruesch in Springdale, Utah, on September 17, 1896. He married Edna Crawford on December 22, 1920, and the couple had a son named Junius. A second child was born to Hyrum and Edna, but as a result of complications with the birth, both Edna and the baby died. On November 12, 1924, Hyrum married Bessie Jolley, daughter of Mary Emma Allred and Robert Donal Jolley, in St. George, Utah. The couple had four children. Bessie died on June 16, 1962, in Las Vegas, Nevada, and Hyrum on June 21, 1965, also in Las Vegas. (Photographs from the Alta J. Halverson collection; courtesy of Denise H. Williams.)

Hyrum's brother, Calvin R. Ruesch, was born to Gottfried and Clara Ruesch on March 30, 1906, in Springdale, Utah. He married Elsa Fredrickson on November 17, 1933. On May 8, 1943, Calvin enlisted as a private in the U.S. Army, later returning to Springdale to work for many years as a heavy equipment operator for the park. He died unexpectedly on October 4, 1976. (Author's collection.)

Elsa Fredrickson Ruesch was born on June 5, 1906, in Vernal, Utah, to Lydia Gertrude Cook and Gustave Fredrickson. She began working for the National Park Service at Zion in 1932, where she met Calvin, another park employee. Elsa was a talented pianist, and several years before her death in 2000, she donated her baby grand piano to the local LDS church, where she had played the organ for many years. (Author's collection.)

John Ruesch, son of Johann and Elisa Ruesch, was born on October 17, 1877, in St. George, Utah. He married Mary Effie Flanigan on August 24, 1898. Effie was born to Ida Johnson and Thomas Emmett Flanigan on February 2, 1881, in Springdale, Utah. They are pictured here with Arnold, the oldest of their eight children. (Courtesy of Della C. Higley.)

John's brother, Walter Ruesch, was born on September 22, 1885, in Springdale, Utah. In 1917, he was appointed custodian of Zion National Park by the federal government, and he spent the majority of his life overseeing the development of the park. This photograph of Walter was taken in 1923 when he was 38 years old. (Courtesy of Flora A. Ruesch.)

On September 30, 1905, Walter Ruesch married Marilla Crawford in St. George, Utah. Marilla was the daughter of early Oak Creek settlers Carnelia Gifford and William Robinson Crawford and was born in Springdale on November 7, 1888. Walter and Marilla had eight children. (Courtesy of Flora A. Ruesch.)

Walter and Marilla Ruesch are pictured here standing in front of the Springdale home built by Walter's father, Johann Jakob Ruesch. Walter and Marilla's son Rupert and his wife, Flora, would eventually live in a house very near to the original Ruesch home. (Courtesy of Flora A. Ruesch.)

This 1908 photograph shows James and Paulina Ruesch Crawford with children. From left to right are Frances, James, Jay, Myrtle (the baby), Paulina, and Nora. Another child, George Leonard, was born before Myrtle, but he died when he was only 19 months old. (Photograph from the Alta J. Halverson collection; courtesy of Denise H. Williams.)

James and Paulina Crawford's children had two sets of grandparents who were early Springdale settlers: James's parents, William and Carnelia Gifford Crawford, and Paulina's parents, Johann and Elisa Spiess Ruesch. Pictured here are, from left to right, Frances, Nora, and Jay in 1905. This photograph was taken by the children's uncle, William Louis Crawford. (Courtesy of Della C. Higley.)

W . L. CRAWFORD, Springdale Utah.

After Nora, Frances, Jay, and Myrtle Crawford (pictured at left from left to right) were born, three more children, Reuben, Della, and Paul, joined James and Paulina's family. Pictured below on the left is Paul Crawford as a baby. Paulina died on May 9, 1916, at the age of 36, just nine days after Paul was born. James Crawford later married Ellen Bean from Franklin, Tennessee. Ellen died on February 11, 1968, and James died just 11 days later on February 22. One of James and Paulina's grandchildren, Alta Jolley Halverson, remembered her grandfather as being "a very shy person" and that "it was really hard to get him to talk." But, "His wife [Ellen] talked constantly," Alta said, "so I guess he didn't need to." (Left, courtesy of Della C. Higley; below, photograph from the Alta J. Halverson collection, courtesy of Denise H. Williams.)

James and Paulina Crawford's daughter Nora (pictured right) was born on February 23, 1903, in Springdale, Utah. While working at Wylie Camp in Zion, one of the area's earliest tourist accommodations, Nora met park employee Donal Jones Jolley. He remembered, "When I got to Springdale and saw Nora I thought she was a cute little kid. I thought she was too young for me but I discovered she was quite grown up so I kept after her." On November 15, 1921, Nora Crawford married Donal in St. George, Utah. The couple's wedding portrait is shown below. (Photographs from the Alta J. Halverson collection; courtesy of Denise H. Williams.)

Donal Jones Jolley was born in Mount Carmel, Utah, on April 26, 1895, to Robert Donal Jolley and Mary Emma Allred. In 1919, Donal began working at the newly created Zion National Park. He later became the first chief ranger of the park. (Photograph from the Alta J. Halverson collection; courtesy of Denise H. Williams.)

After their marriage, Donal and Nora moved into a new house that Donal and his father had built in Springdale. Their daughter Alta, who was born in the home on September 16, 1923, remembered it as being "a small house with four rooms on the main floor and some space in the attic." (Photograph from the Alta J. Halverson collection; courtesy of Denise H. Williams.)

The Jolley children enjoyed growing up with Zion National Park as their playground. Alta remarked, "It seemed like the sun was always shining in Zion." Pictured here are Jolley children Alta (back row, second from left), Lorna (to the right of Alta), and Don (first row, second from left) with some friends. (Photograph from the Alta J. Halverson collection; courtesy of Denise H. Williams.)

Donal Jolley's parents, Robert Donal and Mary Emma Allred Jolley, were married on September 4, 1891, in St. George, Utah. Robert was from Mount Carmel, Utah, and Mary Emma was from Shunesburg, Utah. When they were courting, Robert would ride his horse 30 miles from Mount Carmel to Shunesburg for a visit. (Photograph from the Alta J. Halverson collection; courtesy of Denise H. Williams.)

Mary Emma Allred Jolley's father, John Jones Allred, was a doctor in Shunesburg, Utah. He was born on September 1, 1821, and died on March 16, 1897. It was from his grandfather John Jones Allred that Donal Jones Jolley received his middle name. (Photograph from the Alta J. Halverson collection; courtesy of Denise H. Williams.)

Pictured here is Mary Emma Jolley with her son Forest, who was born on August 1, 1913. Donal Jolley recorded that two of his brothers died during the flu epidemic of 1918—Forest on June 5 and Gerald on September 21. He remembered, "Everywhere you went people were dying." (Photograph from the Alta J. Halverson collection; courtesy of Denise H. Williams.)

Donal Jolley's sister Ivy Pearl married Austin Gifford on October 21, 1919, in St. George, Utah. They are pictured here with their daughter Joy Gifford. Austin Gifford's grandfather Samuel Kendall Gifford was the first of the Gifford family to settle in Springdale. (Photograph from the Alta J. Halverson collection; courtesy of Denise H. Williams.)

Pictured here is the Jolley family, including young Donal (back row, far left), with his grandmother Mary Young Bridgeman (seated, center), widow of John Jones Allred. Mary Young Bridgeman was born in Coal Grove, Ohio, in 1837 and died in Lovell, Wyoming, in 1918. (Photograph from the Alta J. Halverson collection; courtesy of Denise H. Williams.)

These photographs show several Jolley and Gifford children as young adults at Zion National Park sometime around 1920. Above, from left to right are Ivy Jolley Gifford, Austin Gifford, Lula Belle Gifford Seegmiller, Donal Jolley, Joy Jolley Gifford, Jay Gifford, and Alta Gifford. Donal Jolley remembered, "Many of the people who used to work in the park would go up Oak Creek Canyon where there was a beautiful place to have parties, picnics, games and fun together." (Above, photograph from the Alta J. Halverson collection, courtesy of Denise H. Williams; below, photograph by William L. Crawford, courtesy of J. L. Crawford.)

On August 15, 1902, Alvin Carl Hardy was born to George and Sarah Ellen Hunt Hardy in St. George, Utah. On May 15, 1923, in St. George, he married Della Humphries from Virgin City, Utah. Della, born on March 20, 1908, was the daughter of Sarah Isom and Joseph William Humphries. Alvin and Della had five children. In 1927, Alvin Hardy traveled to Springdale looking for work. He decided to settle his family in the town at the gateway to Zion and opened a market. In 1939, the market moved to its location along the main road through Springdale. Though Alvin and Della were not originally from Springdale, their family became a fixture in its society and contributed to its economy, growth, and development. (Courtesy of Nellie H. Ballard.)

Alvin and Della's daughter, Nellie Hardy Ballard, remembered these two photographs as being of the Springdale road leading to their home. As Zion National Park became more well known, a change in Springdale's landscape was evident as roads through town were improved. In the picture above, wagon ruts can be seen in the dirt road, whereas below, the smooth road surface indicates that by this time cars had arrived in Springdale. Electric power lines can also be seen in the photograph below. After the first car drove through the canyon in 1912, Alta Jolley Halverson recalled "counting cars" as one of the activities the youth of Springdale enjoyed. (Both, courtesy of Nellie H. Ballard.)

Pictured above in 1936 is the Springdale home built by Alvin and his father, George Hardy. Alvin and Della's children Nellie and Mack are standing on the front porch with the backdrop of Zion's mountains in the distance. (Courtesy of Nellie H. Ballard.)

This 1938 photograph shows the Springdale Mercantile, along Zion Boulevard in Springdale, owned by Alvin C. Hardy. Nellie Ballard remembered that during the difficult years of the Great Depression, her father would allow townspeople to purchase groceries on credit because he knew they could not afford to buy food for their families. (Courtesy of Nellie H. Ballard.)

By 1942, the storefront of the Springdale Mercantile had slightly changed, and Springdale's U.S. Post Office had been added in the back of the store. As a teenager, Nellie Ballard worked at the post office in her father's store and remembered this as the place where she learned to adopt the responsible practices of a working adult. (Courtesy of Nellie H. Ballard.)

By 1958, Alvin Hardy's store had expanded and was known by the name of Hardy's Market. The post office was still located in the back of the store at that time. The Hardy family represented the industry, frugality, and generosity of Springdale's residents. (Courtesy of Nellie H. Ballard.)

Since its earliest days, Springdale evidenced the ingenuity and craftsmanship of its citizens. This 19th-century photograph shows the chair factory owned by Samuel Kendall Gifford, Carnelia Gifford Crawford's father. (Photograph from the William L. Crawford collection; courtesy of J. L. Crawford.)

The most valuable resource in Springdale was water. In 1893, construction began on the Hurricane Canal as an attempt to harness the power of the Virgin River. Pictured here in 1897 at LaVerkin Hot Springs are canal crew members, from left to right, Sam Crawford, Bishop Hunter, Jess Lemmon, Joe Fames, Alfred Jones, and John Hirschi. (Photograph from the William L. Crawford collection; courtesy of J. L. Crawford.)

A prime example of the ingenuity that abounded among early Zion Canyon settlers was the canyon cable works. As settlers quickly used readily available timber in the construction of homes, fences, and public buildings, it became necessary to find another means of obtaining lumber. In 1900, David Flanigan had an idea to construct a pulley system at the top of one of the mountain peaks, which could then be used to transport timber down the canyon. According to a historical survey of the cable works, the first structure, pictured here, contained a 12-foot-high by 8.5-foot-wide cribbing of sawn, squared timbers—each measuring 10 inches in diameter. This cribbing was joined together by dowels and contained a pulley over which the cable wire ran. The pulley had two tracks for the wire, and a braking mechanism was located about 30 feet to the side of the structure. (Courtesy of Nellie H. Ballard.)

The second documented cable works structure was also built of hand-hewn timber, but the bracing and other parts of the framework were constructed of sawn lumber. The new cable structure contained a large platform for the cable operator and had a smaller, manually operated pulley that was used to haul lumber to the platform, where it could be loaded in baskets and sent down the canyon. In 1901, test runs began at the cable works, as Flanigan sought to entice investors. Initially using 50,000 feet of wire and spending two years perfecting a pulley system, by December 1906, David Flanigan had successfully transferred 200,000 feet of sawed lumber down the 3,000-foot descent to the canyon floor. Farmers also used the cable works to transport produce down the canyon. (Photograph from the William L. Crawford collection; courtesy of J. L. Crawford.)

The framework of the cable system changed several times, as it was often hit by lightning. Pictured here are C. Y. Rozencrans (left) and Louis Crawford (right) on the third documented cable works structure. Several tragedies occurred at the cable works. On July 28, 1908, a group of Springdale youth went to visit Lionel Stout, who was working at the cable works. Clarinda Langston, Thornton Hepworth Jr., and Lionel Stout were standing at the edge of the frame looking down the canyon when lightning struck. Clarinda Langston, the only one of the three to survive, remembered, "I did not know what was happening and I went blind and couldn't see." Others spread a quilt under a tree, put Clarinda on it, and discovered that the two boys were dead. Their bodies were taken down the mountain using the cable works. (Photograph by Putnam and Valentine, Los Angeles, California, from the William L. Crawford collection; courtesy of J. L. Crawford.)

The first living passenger to be transported on the cable works was the Flanigans' dog. David Flanigan's brother William, who assisted in the construction of the edifice, recorded that the dog "made the trip up the wire on September 20, and emerged 'real scart.'" The next evening, when the family returned to the cable, "the dog ran back to camp and never came close to the cable basket again." Pictured here at the top of the cable works are, from left to right, Bertah Cottam, Joseph Webb, Louis Crawford, Maggie Petty, Charles Petty, and Ida Barber Crawford. Pictured below is the Louis Crawford family on a road in the vicinity of what came to be known as Cable Mountain. (Photographs from the William L. Crawford collection; courtesy of J. L. Crawford.)

In September 1904, David Flanigan, with the assistance of his father and brothers William, Ren, and Aaron, purchased the Rube Jolley sawmill, located near Mount Carmel. They moved the sawmill to Zion, near the cable, and began operations there on December 31, 1904. Pictured here, in the winter (at left) and the summer (below), are the buildings at the steam-driven sawmill. The buildings were meant to protect the machinery from the elements. The proximity to the cable wire doubled the output capacity of the mill, but work there was difficult. William Flanigan recorded, "Hauling lumber out of Zion and to St. George, working in storms, is making of us boys, old men." (Photographs by William L. Crawford; courtesy of J. L. Crawford.)

In 1907, David Flanigan sold the cable works to O. D. Gifford and William R. Crawford. Alfred P. Stout operated the sawmill, continuing to process lumber from the vast yellow pine forest at the top of the mountain. Some of the families from town spent the summer up at the mill. Pictured above are the Crawford and Winder children sitting on a small car used to move lumber around the mill. Pictured below is Louis Crawford hauling lumber between the sawmill and the cable. The cable and mill were heavily used until the last load of lumber was transported down the canyon in 1926. In 1929, the wires were removed from the cable works. (Photographs from the William L. Crawford collection; courtesy of J. L. Crawford.)

Community residents began constructing roads in the late 1860s, but muddy conditions often limited access to the canyon. Louis Crawford wrote on February 2, 1909, "Working on the Zion Road. We got the washout fixed so a wagon can be taken over it, but hardly ready for heavy loads." (Photograph by William L. Crawford; courtesy of J. L. Crawford.)

In 1916, the first federal aid road act was passed, and Utah senator Reed Smoot successfully petitioned Congress for $15,000 to "construct an inter-state wagon road or highway through the Mukuntuweap National Monument, Utah." Pictured here is the Higbee Road Crew, from left to right: Edwin Higbee, Dan Dennett, Loren Higbee, Ernest Duffin, Elwood McGee, Sam Christensen, and Walter Ruesch. (Photograph by William L. Crawford; courtesy of J. L. Crawford.)

Edwin Higbee was the contractor in charge of road construction in the park. Pictured again is the Higbee Road Crew in 1916, paving the way for cars to traverse Zion Canyon. In 1923, construction began on the first road to extend all the way from the mouth of the canyon up to the Temple of Sinawava. (Photograph by William L. Crawford; courtesy of J. L. Crawford.)

As roads and irrigation techniques improved and more settlers arrived in and around Springdale, the Virgin River valley became a fruitful farmland. Pictured here in 1918 is a hardworking family harvesting cane in Oak Creek. (Photograph by William L. Crawford; courtesy of J. L. Crawford.)

Through the persistence of its founding families, and the nourishment of the Virgin River, the arid region produced various crops—sustaining life in the desert. Workers used horses to operate farm equipment, as seen in this photograph of a group threshing grain near John Gifford's property. (Courtesy of Nellie H. Ballard.)

Pictured here is the area north of the Alvin C. Hardy home where the Hyrum Ruesch house was located. Nellie Ballard fondly remembered her childhood in Springdale, clearing off an area for a baseball diamond near this road and building a clubhouse in a wash next to the hill on the right. (Courtesy of Nellie H. Ballard.)

Zion Canyon was a vast landscape of possibility with its jagged mountain cliffs, hidden canyons, and deep valleys. The land would never be fully tamed, but the pioneering spirit of the original Mormon settlers opened up the canyon's wonders to the world. Pictured here in a quintessential Western panorama are, from left to right, Barney Gifford, Onnie Dalley, and Ephraim Gifford. (Photograph by William L. Crawford; courtesy of J. L. Crawford.)

Education—both secular and religious—became an important part of the pioneer society in Springdale. School was held in private homes before the construction of the first church building, which was also used as a school. Pictured here in 1915 is a group of students along with teacher Florence Gifford and principal Robert Woodbury (both standing on the right). (Photograph by William L. Crawford; courtesy of J. L. Crawford.)

In 1899, the Springdale schoolchildren posed with principal Willard Hirschi. Alta Jolley Halverson remembered that there were four classrooms in the building with two grades in each room. Each teacher was responsible for teaching two grades. Students attended school in Springdale until eighth grade, after which they went to the high school in Hurricane. (Photograph by William L. Crawford; courtesy of J. L. Crawford.)

In a 1992 interview, Alta Jolley Halverson reminisced about playing outside at the elementary school. She described a game called "the giant stride," where they would hold onto bars at the bottom of some hanging chains, and then they would "run and get the chains going around in a circle." She said, "That was a lot of fun. I guess that must have been dangerous." (Photograph by William L. Crawford; courtesy of J. L. Crawford.)

Pictured here is the 1923 Springdale Latter-day Saints Sunday school. From left to right are (first row, starting with the girl in the checkered dress) Nola Hepworth, Phillip Hepworth, Iona Ruesch, Leora Ruesch, Lucille Gifford, and Allen Ruesch; (second row) Jennie Dennett, Vermont Dalley, Raymond Gifford, Chloe Winder, Nellie Dennett, Laveta Dennett, Clara Hepworth Ruesch, Ruby Higley, Leata Crawford, Victor Ruesch, Daniel Crawford, Carl Gifford, Elmer Higley, Gerald Gifford, and Vilate Crawford; (third row) Lavinnia Gifford, William Gifford, Marilla Ruesch, Jane Hepworth Gifford, Althera Gifford holding Aleatha Gifford, Etta Gifford, Maggie Bean, Ellen Crawford, Mary Jane Crawford, Edith Hepworth, Isaac Langston, Priscilla Hepworth, Ben McBride, Freeborn D. Gifford, Othell Gifford, Cecil Hepworth, Junius Ruesch being held by Orin Ruesch, and Eliel Winder; (fourth row) Barney Gifford, Virgie Christensen, Ethel Gifford, Emma Hepworth Gifford, Oliver D. Gifford, and Esther Gifford; (fifth row) Jesse Gifford, Cornelia Gifford, June Gifford, Samuel Christensen, and Samuel Kendall Gifford; (sixth row) Moses E. Gifford, Thornton Hepworth, Samuel Kendall Gifford, and Moses Elias Gifford Jr.; (seventh row) Squire Crawford, Era Anna Gifford, and Emma Curtis Crawford. (Photograph by William L. Crawford; courtesy of J. L. Crawford.)

The first church building and schoolhouse in Springdale was built prior to World War I. It began as a single-room structure (see photograph above), but in the mid-1920s, an extension was added that contained additional classrooms (below). Unfortunately the church building burned down early in the morning on November 17, 1929. Latter-day Saint ward records were lost, as well as a piano that had just been purchased. Construction began immediately on a new church building and a separate school. The new chapel was completed in 1932 at a cost of $37,000. (Both courtesy of Nellie H. Ballard.)

The contract for construction of a new school building was given to Chester Kemp from St. George. The new school building contained four rooms and two offices. Kemp sponsored a party and dance to celebrate completion of the building, and the school board granted permission to the Church of Jesus Christ of Latter-day Saints to hold church meetings there until the chapel was finished. School enrollment in Springdale had increased considerably because of new jobs being opened up at the national park. In 1929, Paul Thornton began teaching a ninth-grade class, but when the church and school building burned down, it was difficult to find places to hold classes until the new school was finished. Thornton made the most of the situation and, with his students, "put on a very fine operetta although he had only the open air for an opera house." In 1935, the ninth-grade class was moved to the high school in Hurricane, and the eighth grade followed in 1941. (Courtesy of Nellie H. Ballard.)

Though Springdale was a peaceful town, a jail was constructed during the 1930s by the Works Progress Administration. The original structure, pictured here, was built using rock from the cliffs seen behind it. There is no record of anyone actually ever being held overnight in the jail, but J. L. Crawford remembered a close call in 1935. At a town dance, two Civilian Conservation Corps workers had become inebriated. Crawford said that his uncle, "a big strapping guy who was there as a bouncer, swept the floor with them and tossed them down the stairs." The constable came to haul the drunken men off to jail, but other CCC workers intervened and "the town constable was almost killed. He had a brain concussion and his nose was broken. Two of the fellows were later fined," but nobody went to jail as a result of the incident. (Photograph by the author.)

As roads improved and made it easier to access the canyon, and as Zion's natural wonders were publicized throughout the nation, traffic through Springdale began to increase. As a result, a number of businesses were established to cater to the new tourist population. This 1927 photograph shows the Red Crown Gasoline Service Station that was built along Zion Boulevard. (Courtesy of Della C. Higley.)

In 1937, the Utah Oil Company (below) set up a station in Springdale. J. A. Allred ran the service station for a year, after which it was leased by Louis Crawford's son J. L. The next owner was Phillip Hepworth, then Von F. Hoyt and Harold Russell. In the late 1940s, Julius Madsen became the manager. (Courtesy of Nellie H. Ballard.)

As talk of Zion becoming a national park spread through Springdale, a corridor of tourist accommodations, service stations, and restaurants developed along Zion Boulevard. The landscape of the small town was changing. Pictured here is Dewey Excell's Canyon Inn, originally established in 1934 as the West Temple Coffee Shop. (Courtesy of Nellie H. Ballard.)

Times were changing for Springdale and Zion Canyon. It seemed that the pioneering spirit was evolving into one of entrepreneurial foresight. Yet the simple pleasures of a childhood in Springdale, exhibited by Louis Crawford's children, from left to right, J. L., Lloyd, and Elva as they played in the family garden, have always remained an important part of the town's history. (Photograph by William L. Crawford; courtesy of J. L. Crawford.)

Three

ZION

Artist and topographer Frederick S. Dellenbaugh first saw Zion Canyon in the 1870s. He returned to the area in 1903 to paint the landscape, and in 1904, his paintings were displayed at the St. Louis World's Fair. People thought Dellenbaugh had merely painted a fantastical dreamscape, for surely such a beautiful place could not be real. The paintings were also printed in the January 1904 *Scribner's Magazine* along with an article that quoted Dellenbaugh as saying, "Never before has such a naked mountain or rock entered into our minds! Without a shred of disguise its transcendent form rises preeminent. There is almost nothing to compare to it. Niagara has the beauty of energy; the Grand Canyon, of immensity; the Yellowstone, of singularity; the Yosemite, of altitude; the ocean, of power; this Great Temple, of eternity." Thus the national fame of the canyon was born.

Curious travelers began making their way to Utah to see the "Great Temple" of Dellenbaugh's paintings. National publicity surrounding the natural wonders of the canyon prompted Pres. William Howard Taft to issue an executive order on July 31, 1909, officially creating Mukuntuweap National Monument. With this recognition came federal funds to improve roads, and eventually the Union Pacific Railroad stepped in to increase access to the park.

Mormon pioneer Isaac Behunin is generally credited with giving the name "Zion" to the canyon. Zion was a term used by Latter-day Saints to describe a place of peace where they could gather to worship God in their own way—a place that constantly seemed to evade the persecuted Mormon people. When Isaac Behunin arrived in Springdale in 1862, he is said to have exclaimed, "These are the Temples of God, built without the use of human hands. A man can worship God among these great cathedrals as well as in any man-made church—this is Zion."

On November 20, 1919, Pres. Woodrow Wilson signed a bill officially creating "Zion National Park in the State of Utah." The new name reflected the pioneer heritage and surreal beauty of the canyon.

Establishing tourist accommodations was an important part of preparing for Zion to become a national park. The first such accommodations in the canyon were created by William Wylie and his wife, Mary Wilson, pictured here, who opened the Wylie Way Camp in 1917. Wylie, a schoolteacher from Montana, set up a small complex of wooden-floored tents for tourists. (Courtesy of Flora A. Ruesch.)

The Wylies often employed Springdale youth to work at the tourist camp. Nora Crawford was working at Wylie Camp during the time Donal Jolley was courting her. Donal remembered, "I would call them up and say, 'Could I talk to Nora?' and Mr. Wylie would say, 'You cannot. Nora is busy.' " So he began calling when the Wylies were not there. (Courtesy of Flora A. Ruesch.)

On September 15, 1920, the dedication of Zion National Park was held. Speakers included Stephen T. Mather, first director of the National Park Service; U.S. senator Reed Smoot; and former Utah governor William Spry, who had been instrumental in gaining national recognition for the park. (Photograph from the Utah Parks Company Collection, Southern Utah University.)

Another speaker at the dedicatory service was Heber J. Grant, president of the Church of Jesus Christ of Latter-day Saints from 1918 to 1945, who was representing Utah governor Simon Bamberger at the event. President Grant was an avid supporter of Zion National Park and a personal friend of National Park Service director Stephen T. Mather. (Photograph from the Utah Parks Company Collection, Southern Utah University.)

Pictured here is the first visitor center and museum at Zion National Park. The building was constructed in 1924 using native sandstone and is the oldest surviving structure in the park. The museum originally opened to the public in 1928. (Photograph from the Alta J. Halverson collection; courtesy of Denise H. Williams.)

Another original building that still stands at Zion is the old sandstone cafeteria, constructed in the 1930s by architect Gilbert Stanley Underwood. The cafeteria served park visitors staying in nearby cabins. The building now functions as the Zion Nature Center, where Junior Ranger programs and other park activities are held. (Courtesy of Nellie H. Ballard.)

This building, constructed from 1923 to 1924, served as the first headquarters of Zion National Park. The park dramatically changed southern Utah's economy, bringing with it new job opportunities. In addition to park positions, people came to the area to be employed in road construction, building development, and engineering projects. (Courtesy of Nellie H. Ballard.)

Zion's fame quickly spread, and on June 27, 1923, Pres. Warren G. Harding visited the park. He was met at the park entrance by mounted rangers and an orchestra from Dixie College in St. George. The president even took part in a horseback ride to the base of Cable Mountain. Pictured here is the sign located at the east entrance to the park. (Author's collection.)

In 1923, Bryce Canyon, located 70 miles northeast of Zion, was designated as a national monument. Thus, the construction of an extensive road system increasing access to Utah's scenic sites became a priority for early park employees. The result was the Zion–Mount Caramel Highway, along which the east entrance to the park, pictured left, was located. (Photograph from the Alta J. Halverson collection; courtesy of Denise H. Williams.)

Pictured here atop his horse in Echo Canyon, John Winder was responsible for assisting federal surveyors in choosing a feasible route for a new highway. Winder, who owned a ranch along the East Rim, had developed the first livestock trail in the park using the remnants of an old Paiute footpath. (Photograph by William L. Crawford; courtesy of J. L. Crawford.)

William Heep's cabin (pictured above), considered to be one of the earliest cabins in the canyon, was later joined by a number of cabins constructed in Zion National Park by the Utah Parks Company. As park visitation steadily increased during the 1920s, the Utah Parks Company purchased the Wylie Way Camp in 1927 and began constructing its own tourist accommodations. This 1930 photograph (right) shows Ruby Higley and her husband, Henry Miller, in front of these small tourist cabins. According to Angus Woodbury, "Reports from elated visitors, improvement of roads and accommodations and consistent advertising all resulted in vastly increased travel." (Both, courtesy of Della C. Higley.)

Park employees began to lay out a series of trails through the canyon. In 1925, a one-mile footpath was established from the Temple of Sinawava to the Narrows, where the canyon walls close in to leave room only for the river. Pictured on that trail in 1929 is a group of ranger-led tourists observing Zion's "hanging gardens." (Courtesy of the National Park Service History Collection, Harpers Ferry Center.)

Guided horseback trips became popular at Zion during the 1920s. Along the trail to Angels Landing, a series of switchbacks was constructed to make ascension up the steep mountain easier for horses and hikers. The switchbacks were named "Walter's Wiggles" in honor of Walter Ruesch, who oversaw the creation of the West Rim Trail in 1924. (Photograph from the Utah Parks Company Collection, Southern Utah University.)

Springdale native Walter Ruesch, who started out in 1916 as a laborer in charge of equipment in Mukuntuweap National Monument, became "custodian" of the area in 1918. He later served as acting superintendent of the newly created Zion National Park from 1919 to 1925. Over the ensuing years, he held several different titles but was constant as a caretaker of the park. Supt. Eivand T. Scoyen paid tribute to Walter in an article written for the National Park Service publication, the *Courier*. He said, "Walt was an able organizer and unbelievably ingenious in finding means to accomplish a job when invention was the only resource available. If a grading system is ever devised to measure and rate pioneering accomplishment then the Ruesches will certainly rate at the top. Loyal, uncomplaining workers that cared not at all for the hours or difficulties, they contributed so much to the development of Zion National Park that they must not be forgotten." (Courtesy of Flora A. Ruesch.)

In 1923, Walter and his wife, Marilla, attended a conference for park superintendents at Yellowstone National Park. Ralph O. Yardley, reporter and cartoonist, was assigned by the *Stockton Record* to record the activities of the conference. He sketched this likeness of Walter Ruesch, which was published on February 9, 1924. (Courtesy of Flora A. Ruesch.)

WALTER RUESCH WAS BORN AND REARED IN UTAHS DIXIELAND AND HA BEEN IN CHARGE OF GORGEOUSLY COLORED ZION CANYON EVER SINCE IT WAS FIRST MADE A NATIONAL MONUMENT.

On May 15, 1909, Rupert Ruesch was born to Walter and Marilla Ruesch at their family home in Springdale. Pictured here as a young man at the Wylie Way Camp, Rupert spent many years working at the park and also served a mission to Germany for the LDS Church before marrying Flora Anderson. (Courtesy of Flora A. Ruesch.)

In 1918, Walter Ruesch asked Donal Jones Jolley if he would be interested in working at Zion National Park. Donal was interested and submitted an application. He was hired by the National Park Service and remembered, "While I was working in Zion in the early days of the park I was a foreman helping to make the East and West Rim Trails." In 1927, when Walter Ruesch was appointed as the general foreman of the park, Donal Jolley was made chief ranger of Zion National Park. (Photographs from the Alta J. Halverson collection; courtesy of Denise H. Williams.)

Ranger Jolley's duties changed when the number of visitors increased and cars regularly traveled through the park, but in the early days of his post, he primarily patrolled the park boundaries on horseback and worked to develop trails and roads through the park. (Photograph from the Alta J. Halverson collection; courtesy of Denise H. Williams.)

Donal and Nora Jolley had four children after the death of their first child in 1922. Pictured here is their second child, Alta, who was five years old when her father became the chief ranger. She remembered Zion as "a fun place to live." (Photograph from the Alta J. Halverson collection; courtesy of Denise H. Williams.)

Sisters Venus (left) and Alta Jolley posed for this July 1926 photograph. Alta recorded that as children growing up in the park, they enjoyed hiking in the hills behind their house and learning to swim in the Virgin River. (Photograph from the Alta J. Halverson collection; courtesy of Denise H. Williams.)

When Donal Jolley became chief ranger in 1927, he and his family moved into a government house inside the park. He said, "We were happy in the new home. It had three bedrooms and was made of sandstone blocks eighteen inches thick." Pictured here are sisters Alta (left) and Lorna Jolley in front of the home. (Photograph from the Alta J. Halverson collection; courtesy of Denise H. Williams.)

The Jolley children—Alta, Lorna, Venus, and Don—enjoyed spending their childhood at Zion. While they could play with visiting dogs and cats, park regulations prevented them from having such pets while living inside park boundaries. They did, however, have a pet mountain sheep. Donal Jolley recorded, "I was getting some cattle and the ewe was with them. She followed my horse home. We had maple floors with Navajo rugs covering them. The ewe would jump on a rug and skid across the room." The children also had two baby cougars as pets as well as a family of ring-tailed cats in the attic. (Photographs from the Alta J. Halverson collection; courtesy of Denise H. Williams.)

Pictured with the snowman are, from left to right, Lorna, Alta, Venus, and Don in 1934. Alta later recalled that there were three stone houses in the park at that time, all located near the park entrance. The Jolley family lived in one house, and the park superintendent lived in another of the homes. (Photograph from the Alta J. Halverson collection; courtesy of Denise H. Williams.)

Pictured from left to right, Alta, Don, Venus, Agnes Gifford (cousin to the Jolley children), and Lorna posed for this 1936 photograph. The Jolleys had originally intended to name their son Donal Park, since he was born in the park, but they heard that other families in the area had named their boys Park, so they named him Donal Clark instead. (Photograph from the Alta J. Halverson collection; courtesy of Denise H. Williams.)

Alta Jolley Halverson remembered climbing to the top of Lady Mountain with her father. She sat down and dangled her feet over the side of the cliff, but her father immediately pulled her to safety and issued a stern lecture on the dangers of getting too close to the edge. Pictured here is the steep trail up Lady Mountain. (Photograph from the Alta J. Halverson collection; courtesy of Denise H. Williams.)

Children of park employees and other Springdale town residents attended high school 21 miles away in Hurricane. Pictured here in 1940 are Alta Jolley (second row, third from right) and her classmates in front of the school bus that would transport them to and from Hurricane. (Photograph from the Alta J. Halverson collection; courtesy of Denise H. Williams.)

The first high school graduating class in Hurricane, Utah, graduated in 1928. There was no school building in the town at that time, so coursework was completed at the home of a local teacher. During the Great Depression of the 1930s, federal funding was granted to the Works Progress Administration for the construction of a two-story, red-brick high school building in Hurricane. The building, pictured above, opened just after Thanksgiving in 1936. Alta Jolley graduated from Hurricane High School on May 19, 1941. Pictured below is the Springdale school bus in Hurricane, Utah, on April 8, 1938. (Photographs from the Alta J. Halverson collection; courtesy of Denise H. Williams.)

Various generations of park employees, their families, and others who grew up in Springdale looked upon their teenage years as being, according to Alta Jolley Halverson (pictured on the right above), "a good age for a lot of people." High school dances, picnics in the canyon, and other activities occupied the time of the area's youth. Della Crawford Higley (right), pictured at left with her friend Dorothy Giles at Weeping Rock in Zion Canyon, said of Springdale, "It was a wonderful place to grow up." (Above photograph from the Alta J. Halverson collection, courtesy of Denise H. Williams; left, courtesy of Della C. Higley.)

Donal Jolley, pictured here in between friends Chambers (left) and Hanson (right), remembered having a Halloween party on the night Orson Wells broadcast his story "War of the Worlds." According to Donal, he and his friends had listened long enough to find out that it was not true, but many others "panicked and just got in their cars and left not knowing where they were going." (Photograph from the Alta J. Halverson collection; courtesy of Denise H. Williams.)

Zion National Park not only provided opportunities for fun and recreation but also for employment. Pictured here in a 1931 promotional picture for the Ford Motor Company is a group of National Park Service employees behind the original visitor center. (Photograph from the Alta J. Halverson collection; courtesy of Denise H. Williams.)

Zion National Park staff members are pictured here in 1940. From left to right are (first row) Arden Schiefer, Fred Brueck, Harold Russell, Fred Fagergren, Donal Jolley, Merle Walker, John M. Davis, and Supt. Preston P. Patraw; (second row) Katherine Schram, Harry Brockmeier, Harlan Stevenson, Tom Foley, Art DeMille, Walter Ruesch, and Allen Strunk. (Photograph from the Alta J. Halverson collection; courtesy of Denise H. Williams.)

The author's grandfather Hal Taylor is pictured seated in the center of the fourth row in this 1950s Zion National Park staff photograph. Ranger Taylor and his family enjoyed living in a government home at the east entrance to the park, although rattlesnakes were occasional and unwelcome houseguests. (Courtesy of Flora A. Ruesch.)

·UNITED STATES·
𝔇epartment of the Interior
LIFETIME PASS

Elsa F. Ruesch

THE HOLDER OF THIS PASS AS A RETIRED EMPLOYEE OF THE DEPARTMENT OF THE INTERIOR, OR SURVIVING SPOUSE OF SUCH EMPLOYEE, WILL BE ADMITTED FREE TO ANY UNRESTRICTED AREA UNDER JURISDICTION OF THE DEPARTMENT.

No. 1871

SECRETARY OF THE INTERIOR

This Department of the Interior lifetime admission pass was issued to Zion National Park employee Elsa F. Ruesch on November 15, 1961. The pass was signed on the front by Secretary of the Interior Stewart Udall and on the back by National Park Service director Conrad L. Wirth. Elsa served for many years as the secretary to the superintendent of Zion. (Author's collection.)

Park employees had various duties, such as road and trail construction, bridge and building construction, wildlife management, and visitor assistance. In May 1932, a severe storm ravaged the canyon, blocking the main road with mud, trees, and boulders. Walter Ruesch summoned all park workers at 3:00 a.m. to clear the road so tourist activities could continue uninterrupted in the morning. (Courtesy of Flora A. Ruesch.)

The original custodian of Zion National Park was Walter Ruesch, and the first official superintendent was Richard T. Evans. The next superintendent was Eivand T. Scoyen, who was followed by Thomas J. Allen. Preston P. Patraw was next, followed by C. M. Finnan, who was replaced by Paul Franke. Through all of the changes in administration, Walter Ruesch carried on the work of developing and caring for the park until his retirement in 1948. (Courtesy of Flora A. Ruesch.)

To meet the needs of the growing number of tourists, additional accommodations, restaurants, and stores appeared in Springdale. The pictured tourist camp and store was established by Ivy Jolley Gifford and was later owned by Julius V. Madsen. It was located where Bumbleberry Inn is today. (Courtesy of Nellie H. Ballard.)

This 1926 photograph shows Allred's Camp along Zion Boulevard, which included a complex of tourist cabins, a general store, and a café. The establishment was founded by Alvin Allred from Mount Carmel in 1921. It was located where Pioneer Lodge is today. (Courtesy of Nellie H. Ballard.)

In 1932, Clarence Olson built a few cabins and called the place Olson Camp. He later increased the number of cabins on the property, which, in 1951, was purchased by Hal Taylor. The Taylor family subsequently moved to Kanab and sold the Olson Motel, which later became present-day Canyon Ranch Motel. This photograph of Olson Camp was taken in 1940. (Courtesy of Nellie H. Ballard.)

On March 4, 1930, Dewy Excell arrived in Springdale to work for the National Park Service. In 1932, he purchased some land, and by 1934, he opened a small café called the West Temple Coffee Shop (above). It was later operated by Austin and Venice Excell and was called Canyon Inn (below). A 1947 history of Springdale noted, "They have fed famous people there. In 1946, a company from Hollywood made the picture 'Ramrod,' in Zion Canyon and Joel McCrea, Preston Foster and Veronica Lake often ate at Canyon Inn." (Both courtesy of Nellie H. Ballard.)

In 1934, Alvin Allred replaced his original tourist camp buildings with a larger stone building that housed the café, store, and the office for the tourist cabins. Allred's new building, pictured here, later became the Pioneer Restaurant, which is still located in the same stone structure on Zion Boulevard. (Courtesy of Nellie H. Ballard.)

During the 1940s, a man named John Dratter from Helper, Utah, bought a piece of property from Henry Wilson in Springdale. He established the Dratter Motel, which began with 10 former National Park Service cabins that were moved to Zion Boulevard and used to create the complex seen here. It became a popular place for tourists to stay. (Courtesy of Nellie H. Ballard.)

During the 1950s, the name of the Dratter Motel was changed to Zion Rest Motel. A swimming pool and additional cabin accommodations were added at that time. The motel later became Flanigan's Inn, which stands on the property today. (Courtesy of Nellie H. Ballard.)

Early Springdale's quiet past was quickly becoming history as the town grew along with the popularity and fame of Zion National Park. Families of tourists from all over the country came to see the park that had, for many years, been enjoyed primarily by local residents such as the Higley and Gifford families, pictured here. (Courtesy of Della C. Higley.)

The Union Pacific Railroad played a large part in promoting and providing access to the national parks of the American West. In 1922, a railroad line was established from Salt Lake City to Cedar City, Utah, where tourists were then transported by bus to Zion National Park. Postcards, such as the one pictured above depicting the view from Observation Point, were printed by Union Pacific. Railroad companies also advertised the scenic wonders of Western national parks in various publications. Zion's Great White Throne was a favorite advertising icon, as seen in the picture at right from a 1946 Union Pacific advertisement that proclaimed, "1708 Square Miles of Scenic Beauty." (Both author's collection.)

WASHINGTON COUNTY FIRST

Washington County has rested long
    From the outside world's invasion,
But now its sung in every song
    It's the beauty spot of our Nation.

We should make a vow right here and now
    To bow our heads no longer,
But have much pride as we work and stride
    To make our county stronger.

For years the world has left us out
    And we have paid the bounty,
Now let's turn loose and give a boost
    For our beautiful Washington County.

DONAL J. JOLLEY.

Park rangers developed programs to teach the public about the natural wonders of Zion Canyon. As early as the mid-1920s, park naturalists took groups of visitors on walks through the park, pointing out rock formations and various types of flora and fauna. Ranger naturalist H. L. Reid would take visitors on relatively strenuous hikes as part of his crusade to cure Americans of what he called the disease "cushionitis." Pictured above is a 1930 nature walk at the Temple of Sinawava, photographed by E. T. Scoyen. At left, chief ranger Donal Jolley, who enjoyed writing poetry, captured the essence of change in Utah's Washington County, where the park is located, which had "rested long from the outside world's invasion." (Above, courtesy of the National Park Service History Collection, Harpers Ferry Center; left, poem from the Alta J. Halverson collection, courtesy of Denise H. Williams.)

Four

BRINGING THE WORLD TO ZION

With Zion National Park's fame spreading all over the world, the small town of Springdale struggled to support the ever increasing influx of tourists. Due to publicity and services provided by the Union Pacific Railroad, visitation at Zion virtually doubled from 8,400 visitors in 1924 to 16,817 in 1925—and the numbers continued to rise. In cooperation with the National Park Service, the Utah Parks Company, a subsidiary of Union Pacific, was incorporated in 1923 to serve as a concessionaire in providing access and accommodation at national parks in Utah and northern Arizona. The Utah Parks Company provided lodging, dining, and transportation facilities at Zion, Bryce Canyon, the Grand Canyon, and Cedar Breaks National Monument. The company, based in Cedar City, Utah, purchased the Wylie Way Camp and commissioned the construction of a lodge, which opened at Zion National Park in 1925.

Since its inception as a national park, transportation into and out of the canyon had always been a problem at Zion. It seemed that the only plausible way to link the canyon with the national parks to the east would be to go through a mountain—literally. Thus, a slew of contractors, miners, engineers, and laborers descended on the canyon to create the 5,613-foot-long Zion–Mount Carmel Tunnel from 1927 to 1930. Newspapers declared the new road from Zion to Mount Carmel to be "one of the world's great highways."

Zion National Park was also the focus of several New Deal programs enacted by Pres. Franklin D. Roosevelt, namely the Civilian Conservation Corps, which set up several camps in the park. As the nation worked to bring itself out of the Great Depression, Zion became a symbol of progress and opportunity. The future looked bright for the park as developments and improvements kept pace with the growing number of tourists.

The Utah Parks Company saw an opportunity to combine Zion National Park, Bryce Canyon National Monument, and the Grand Canyon into one convenient package. In 1924, the company began operating the El Escalante Hotel in Cedar City, and bus tours to all of the region's national parks were organized. In 1925, buses advertised as having "demountable tops for viewing the spectacular canyon walls" were introduced. As part of its movement to open the parks to tourists, the Utah Parks Company oversaw the construction of lodging accommodations at the various parks, one of which was completed at Zion in 1925. The pictures are of the completed lodge, designed and constructed by architect Gilbert Stanley Underwood. (Above, courtesy of Flora A. Ruesch; below, photograph by William L. Crawford, courtesy of J. L. Crawford.)

When presented with the Utah Parks Company's original plans to construct a large hotel within Zion's boundaries, National Park Service director Stephen T. Mather was opposed to the idea, preferring what he believed would be a less-obtrusive cluster of small cabins. He soon relented, however, and agreed to the construction of a larger hotel unit in addition to a number of smaller guest cabins. The completed lodge, a two-story frame building with a hipped roof, portico, and second-story terrace on stone piers, was a classic example of Gilbert Stanley Underwood's "rustic" style of architecture. On May 18, 1925, a large celebration commemorated the grand opening of the lodge. There were a reported 1,152 visitors in attendance for the festivities. (Above, courtesy of Nellie H. Ballard; below, photograph from the Alta J. Halverson collection, courtesy of Denise H. Williams.)

In 1928, it was reported that a record 30,016 visitors came to Zion. According to a local newspaper, visitors came from "every state in the Union, District of Columbia, and the Territories of Hawaii and Alaska" as well as the foreign countries of Australia, Bolivia, Canada, England, France, Germany, South Africa, and Sweden. Park statistics showed that 25,031 visitors arrived by automobile; 4,940 arrived on Union Pacific buses; and 45 visitors arrived by horseback, wagon, and other miscellaneous means of travel. In 1929, Union Pacific spent $151,000 on improvements to Zion Lodge. (Photographs from the Alta J. Halverson collection; courtesy of Denise H. Williams.)

Unfortunately the original Zion Lodge burned down on January 28, 1966, after a fire was started accidentally by a crew using blowtorches to remove and replace some old vinyl flooring at the lodge. Union Pacific and National Park Service employees fought the blaze using a pumper truck, but by the time the fire was put out, only the sandstone pillars and fireplace remained. Thus, the only original park lodging facilities were several of Underwood's guest cabins. (Above, courtesy of Nellie H. Ballard; below, photograph from the Utah Parks Company Collection, Southern Utah University.)

From the ashes of the original Zion Lodge arose a new building, constructed in just 100 days, minimizing the fire's effect on tourist activities in the park. Having been built in such haste, however, the new lodge looked very different from the original. In 1992, a historic renovation project restored the look of the lodge to match Gilbert Stanley Underwood's original structure. The difference between the 1966 reconstruction (above) and the original lodge (below) is illustrated here. (Above, courtesy of Nellie H. Ballard; below, courtesy of the National Park Service History Collection, Harpers Ferry Center.)

This view, from a 1930 color-applied lantern slide, shows the complex of park buildings from the top of Lady Mountain. The lodge can be seen on the left end of the cluster. Other buildings included guest cabins, constructed beginning in 1927 with flushboard walls and stone corner chimneys; a women's dormitory, completed in 1927; a swimming pool and bathhouse, completed in 1928; a stable, completed in 1929; and a number of other park administrative buildings and employee housing units. An accompanying cafeteria building would not be constructed until 1935. (Courtesy of the National Park Service History Collection, Harpers Ferry Center.)

This 1957 photograph by S. Horace Pickering shows one of the famous "sing-a-ways," when Utah Parks Company lodge employees would sing their farewells to departing tour buses. The sing-a-way tradition carried over from Zion to other national parks. Alta Jolley Halverson remembered lining up and singing songs to departing visitors when she worked at the Grand Canyon. (Courtesy of the National Park Service History Collection, Harpers Ferry Center.)

Pictured here is one of the original employee cabins built between 1927 and 1937. A number of park buildings that went up during the 1930s were built by CCC workers. Though many of these men had little or no architectural experience, they were supervised by resident architects and engineers. Larger ranger dormitories were constructed during the 1940s. (Courtesy of Flora A. Ruesch.)

The Zion Lodge was always a hub of activity. Pictured here are two Utah Parks Company waitresses in front of the employee cabins in 1925. Lodge employees wore different uniforms depending on whether they worked in the guest cabins or the dining room. (Courtesy of Flora A. Ruesch.)

Desmond Owens, a Utah Parks Company bellhop, is pictured here in his park uniform in the late 1920s. He is standing in front of the Zion Lodge store, which supplied tourists with cold drinks, snacks, park maps, and souvenirs. (Courtesy of Flora A. Ruesch.)

The Utah Parks Company was in operation from 1923 to 1973 and employed thousands of college students to work in its restaurants and lodges and to conduct bus tours of the region's national parks. A 1938 newspaper article reported that 95 percent of the 550 Utah Parks Company employees at Zion, Bryce, and the Grand Canyon were from southern Utah and northern Arizona. Pictured above are bellhops at the Zion Lodge. Members of the trio at left are, from left to right, Rupert Ruesch, Lee Chamberlain, and Desmond Owens. (Above, photograph from the Alta J. Halverson collection, courtesy of Denise H. Williams; left, courtesy of Flora A. Ruesch.)

The dining services offered at Zion Lodge immediately became one of the most popular features of the Utah Parks Company operations. In 1926, the Union Pacific Railroad spent $250,000 in improvements to its lodges at Zion and Bryce Canyon National Parks. At Zion, plans were made to double the size of the lodge dining rooms, and kitchen facilities were also enlarged and updated. Pictured here are earlier (above) and later (below) kitchen crews employed at the Zion Lodge. (Above, courtesy of Flora A. Ruesch; below, photograph from the Utah Parks Company Collection, Southern Utah University.)

In addition to new visitor accommodations, new transportation corridors were constructed. This arch bridge spanning Pine Creek was completed in 1930. The idea was conceived by National Park Service landscape architect Harry Langley. The Reynolds-Ely Company, along with Lou Whitney, a bridge builder from Springville, Utah, oversaw the completion of the project. (Courtesy of Nellie H. Ballard.)

While work was being done on the Zion–Mount Carmel Tunnel, road crews were constructing a series of switchbacks up the side of the mountain to allow access to what would become the west portal of the tunnel. In just 3.6 miles, the completed road rose 800 feet in elevation with a maximum grade of six percent. (Courtesy of Nellie H. Ballard.)

At the base of the mountain where the tunnel was being built, temporary housing was constructed for the army of workers. The main company involved in the tunnel project was the Nevada Construction Company from Fallow, Nevada. Two employee casualties occurred during the three-year construction project. (Courtesy of Nellie H. Ballard.)

One-hundred and forty-six tons of dynamite was used in the construction of the tunnel, and 72,000 cubic yards of stone was blasted from the mountain. The resulting 16-foot-high and 22-foot-wide tunnel stretched for 1.06 miles. A 1928 newspaper following the tunnel's progress described section three of the construction process: "This section calls for excavation totaling 140,000 cubic yards in 3½ miles and is classified as 100 percent solid rock." (Courtesy of Nellie H. Ballard.)

An initial "pilot tunnel" was completed on February 13, 1928, running from the east entrance to the west. The dimensions of the pilot tunnel were 8 feet high by 9 feet wide. Crews then began "ring drilling" to expand the tunnel to its full size. A drill was placed onto an iron spindle in the pilot tunnel, and every 3 feet, a series of 17 holes was drilled in the ceiling and walls. Crews would then use dynamite to blast out 36 feet of full bore tunnel. Unique features of the tunnel, which opened on July 4, 1930, included six galleries from which tourists could view the canyon. The original purpose of the galleries was to provide ventilation for tunnel workers. The completed tunnel was an engineering marvel. (Both, courtesy of Nellie H. Ballard.)

In this 1936 photograph, Latter-day Saint church historian Andrew Jensen (left) and William R. Palmer, scholar of Native American traditions and the history of southern Utah, pose at the east entrance to the newly created Zion Tunnel. (Photograph from the Palmer Collection, Southern Utah University.)

In the throes of the Great Depression, Pres. Franklin D. Roosevelt sought to bring the country out of financial recession by putting Americans to work. As part of his "New Deal for America," he launched a series of programs, including, in 1933, the Civilian Conservation Corps. Pictured here is the Bridge Mountain CCC camp, the first of two camps established at Zion National Park. (Courtesy of Nellie H. Ballard.)

The CCC camps brought with them a sense of hope for discouraged Springdale residents. Alta Jolley Halverson remembered, "Nobody had any money in Springdale. It was during Depression times, and hardly anybody had a job most of the time." The second of the CCC camps, pictured here, was referred to as the Watchman Camp. CCC crews were primarily responsible for landscaping projects in the park, constructing buildings and dams to contain the Virgin River, clearing campgrounds, putting up fences, grading roads, and extending the park's trail system. Reports indicated that $180,000 would be circulated into Washington County's economy as a result of the CCC. (Both, courtesy of Flora A. Ruesch.)

The Civilian Conservation Corps employed 2.5 million young men in 1,500 camps, similar to those at Zion, across the country. The camps consisted of military-style barracks and were usually located on federally owned land in areas that would benefit from their labor projects. (Courtesy of Flora A. Ruesch.)

National Park Service employees at Zion worked closely with the CCC units in the planning and execution of projects. Pictured in this 1937 photograph are CCC and NPS employees. From left to right are (first row) unidentified, Einar Strand, Mr. Doerner, and Rupert Ruesch; (second row) two unidentified, Claude Fleming, Ross Rozelle, Fred Fagergren, and A. E. Cowell. (Courtesy of Flora A. Ruesch.)

CCC recruits at the Zion camp were, according to a local newspaper, "Utah boys between the ages of 17 and 23 who are unemployed and single." These two 1937 photographs include National Park Service and CCC employees Einar Strand, Rupert Ruesch, Claude Fleming, Ross W. Rozelle, Fred Fogergren, A. E. Cowell, Donal Jolley, Calvin Ruesch, Charles Gerrard, and Antone Bowler. National Park Service employees helped to supervise CCC workers in masonry, carpentry, plumbing, plastering, and electric wiring projects. It was reported by another newspaper that "all phases of the projects in this park are planned to train the [CCC] boys for employment when their enrollment period expires." (Both, courtesy of Flora A. Ruesch.)

The efforts of workers during the 1930s and 1940s prepared the park for an increased post–World War II tourist influx. Additional improvements were made in the 1960s with the completion of a new park visitor center. Pictured right at the visitor center dedication are, from left to right, Art Bells, Tom Murray, and Bain Matheson. (Photograph from the Utah Parks Company Collection, Southern Utah University.)

"Uncle" Bain Matheson, as he was known to park employees, was famous for his deep pit barbeques and his kind demeanor. Uncle Bain was the chef for the annual employee picnics and special park events. Pictured below is the serving table at the 1960 canyon picnic. (Photograph from the Utah Parks Company Collection, Southern Utah University.)

According to the *Salt Lake Tribune*, Zion National Park was officially "on the tourist bandwagon to stay." Tourism at the park skyrocketed after World War II, with 212,280 visitors in 1946, compared to 78,280 in 1945. By 1950, annual visitation at Zion had reached 323,402. In 1955, when this photograph of tourists Carolyn Smith, Margaret Grooms, and Norman Akita (from left to right) was taken by Theodore F. Whitmoyer, Zion saw an excess of 400,000 visitors. Visitation surpassed 500,000 in 1957; 600,000 in 1961; 700,000 in 1964; 800,000 in 1966; 900,000 in 1969; and 1 million in 1975. The popularity of Zion National Park had caught on like wildfire and continues to spread across the world. (Courtesy of the National Park Service History Collection, Harpers Ferry Center.)

This 1950 photograph shows Marilyn Bowman (left) and other tourists atop Angels Landing. A 1954 study of Utah tourism, which focused primarily on Zion National Park, reported that tourists stayed in the state for an average of 3.4 days and spent an average of $9.70 per day. Ninety-nine percent of visitors surveyed said that they would recommend Utah as a vacation spot. (Photograph from the Utah Parks Collection, Southern Utah University.)

Park employees and visitors alike enjoyed the fruits of Zion National Park's growth and development. Zion was advertised around the world as a "scenic playground." For those who grew up in Springdale, the park literally was their playground; and employees, such as these bellhops who posed for an "old-time" photograph in 1970, Zion was a place to work and play. (Photograph from the Utah Parks Collection, Southern Utah University.)

Zion National Park is a place where history deepens one's appreciation for the natural beauty of the canyon. Visitors marvel at the pioneering spirit of those who created an oasis in the arid desert. In many languages, tourists note their fascination with the engineering of the tunnel and wonder how trails to the remote reaches of the park were constructed. Even when water was scarce and prospects were dim, early Mormon pioneers remained vigilant in their quest to settle at the mouth of Zion Canyon because their leader, Brigham Young, told them that the time would come when "hundreds of thousands will pass through your canyon and they will need you." The majestic wonders of Zion existed long before humans ever set foot in the canyon, yet it was only through the ingenuity and foresight of the area's early settlers that the canyon was opened to the world. (Photograph by William L. Crawford; courtesy of J. L. Crawford.)

SELECTED BIBLIOGRAPHY

Alder, Douglas D. and Karl F. Brooks. *A History of Washington County: From Isolation to Destination.* Springdale, UT: Zion Natural History Association, 2007.

Alter, J. Cecil. *Through the Heart of the Scenic West.* Salt Lake City, UT: Shepard Book Company, 1927.

Crawford, J. L. *Zion Album: A Nostalgic History of Zion Canyon.* Springdale, UT: Zion Natural History Association, 1986.

———. *Zion National Park: Towers of Stone.* Springdale, UT: Zion Natural History Association, 1988.

Crawford/Jolley/Halverson Family Histories. Alta Jolley Halverson Collection. Provo, UT.

Crawford, Nancy C., and Merwin G. Fairbanks. *A Pioneer History of Zion Canyon and Springdale to 1947.* Spanish Fork, UT: J-Mart Publishing Company, 1972.

Department of the Interior, National Park Service Public Use Statistics Office, Annual Park Visitation Reports.

Garate, Donald T. *The Zion Tunnel: From Slickrock to Switchback.* Springdale, UT: Zion Natural History Association, 1989.

Hagood, Allen. *This is Zion.* Salt Lake City, UT: Publishers Press, 1982.

Hafen, Lyman. *Mukuntuweap: Landscape and Story in Zion Canyon, Original Watercolors by Roland Lee.* St. George, UT: Tonaquint Press, 1996.

Ruesch, Rupert. *Life of Walter Ruesch: 1885–1950.* Springdale, UT: self-published, 1980.

Smith-Cavros, Eileen M. *Pioneer Voices of Zion Canyon.* Springdale, UT: Zion Natural History Association, 2006.

Stout, Dell Crawford. *The Family of William Robinson and Carnelia Gifford Crawford.* Hurricane, UT: self-published, 2002.

The Outstanding Wonder: Zion Canyon's Cable Mountain Draw Works. Springdale, UT: Zion Natural History Association, 1981.

Woodbury, Angus M. *A History of Southern Utah and its National Parks.* Salt Lake City, UT: Utah State Historical Society, 1950.

INDEX

ACROSS AMERICA, PEOPLE ARE DISCOVERING SOMETHING WONDERFUL. *THEIR HERITAGE.*

Arcadia Publishing is the leading local history publisher in the United States. With more than 4,000 titles in print and hundreds of new titles released every year, Arcadia has extensive specialized experience chronicling the history of communities and celebrating America's hidden stories, bringing to life the people, places, and events from the past. To discover the history of other communities across the nation, please visit:

www.arcadiapublishing.com

Customized search tools allow you to find regional history books about the town where you grew up, the cities where your friends and family live, the town where your parents met, or even that retirement spot you've been dreaming about.

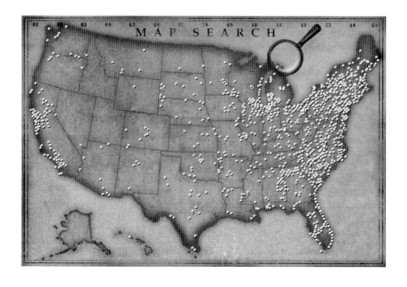